A Big Girl Color Book
A MOUNTAIN IN OUR BACK YARD
THE BIG GIRL COLOR BOOK VI
W. A. WELBOURN

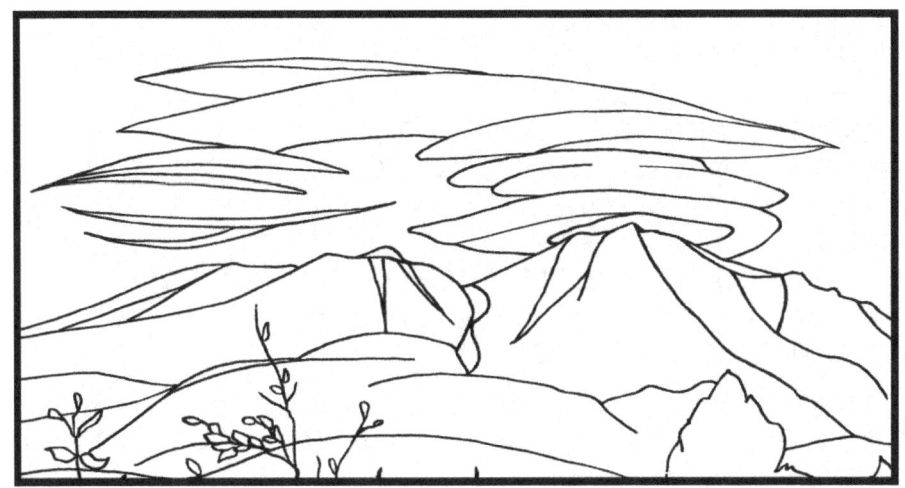

What will you remember about **2020**? For us, and the world, it has been a severe trial with the Covid 19 pandemic. We have had other struggles at home but the weather held off and we got everything back in shape. With the government shelter-at-home order there is a lot more time for art. Friend Janet submitted her favorite, personal mountain photos for my imagination. With her coaxing I realized I had more time to work on the third color book in my Mount Shasta Series!

This color book is dedicated to: My Friendship Garden, so many beautiful flowers (friends) all over the world.

W. A. Welbourn – Mount Shasta
(All Rights Reserved)
with Janet Ackerman Beck

Cover and inset Illustration: Mount Shasta from Sisson Meadow

CONTENTS
(All horizontal format)
P. 5 DILLER CANYON AND LENTICULAR (JANET ACKERMAN BECK IMAGE – USED WITH PERMISSION) (PHOTO)
P. 7 KAHUNA LENTICULAR (PHOTO)
P. 9 DILLER HEART CHAKRA (JANET ACKERMAN BECK IMAGE – USED WITH PERMISSION) (PHOTO)
P. 11 GOLD CLOUD COLUMN (PHOTO)
P. 13 HEART SUPPORT (CONCEPT)
P. 15 MORNING PINKS HALO (PHOTO)
P. 17 PURPLE MOUNTAIN PINK SUNRISE (PHOTO)
P. 19 PURPLE GOLD MOUNTAIN (HOMAGE TO MCCLOUD HIGH) (PHOTO)
P. 21 QUEEN OF OUR HEARTS (CONCEPT)
P. 23 SAND FLAT SKETCH (CONCEPT)
P. 25 MOUNT SHASTA FROM SISSON MEADOW (FALL) (PHOTO)
P. 27 THE TRINITY (EASTER INSPIRATION) (CONCEPT)
P. 29 LOVE YOU TO THE MOON (CONCEPT)

Color!!! *Reduce your stress. Dispell your negative thoughts. Improve your focus. Enter your medatitive coloring state.*

Find a comfortable, quiet spot where you can spend some time. I recommend using colored pencils. If you use wet markers or paints, consider removing the page from the book and using a blotter. There is a page at the end of this book that can be removed and used as a blotter between pages.

Inspiration photos and xoncept drawings are on the back cover of this book.

Janet Ackerman Beck was kind of enough to send images for my use. With her additions, I realized I had only to create a few more images for a third Mount Shasta color book.

Janet and I share Mount Shasta in our back yard. I have a north facing view of both peaks (Shastina and Mount Shasta). Janet's view is from the west and a grand view of Diller Canyon on Shastina Peak. Diller Canyon proper looks so much like a big heart.

If you need more inspiration please visit my links:

www.TBGCB.blogspot.com
(This Google blog uses cookies to track visits)

My facebook page
facebook/TBGCBseries.com

No part of this book may be reproduced without permission of the author.
W. A. Welbourn – Mount Shasta
(All Rights Reserved)

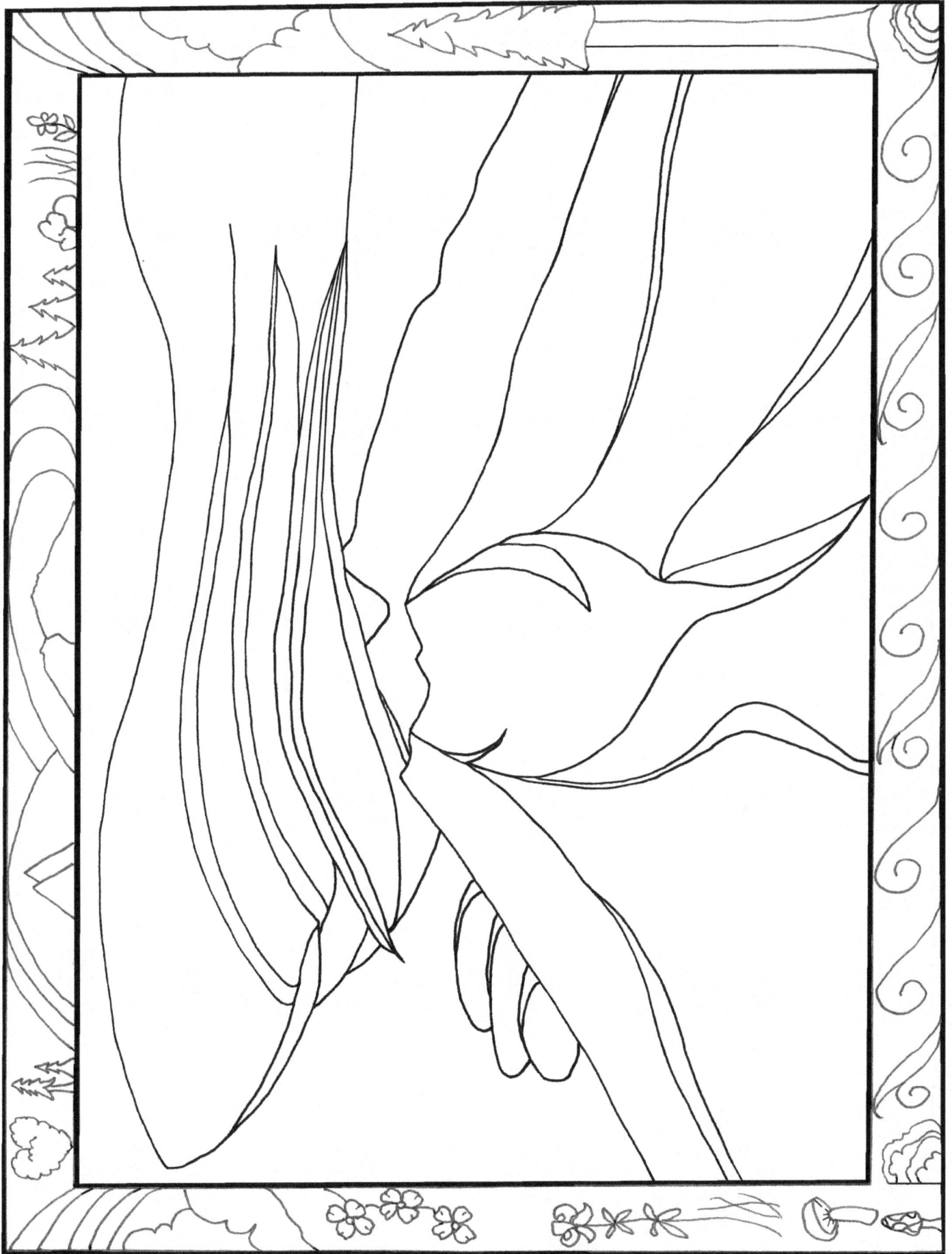

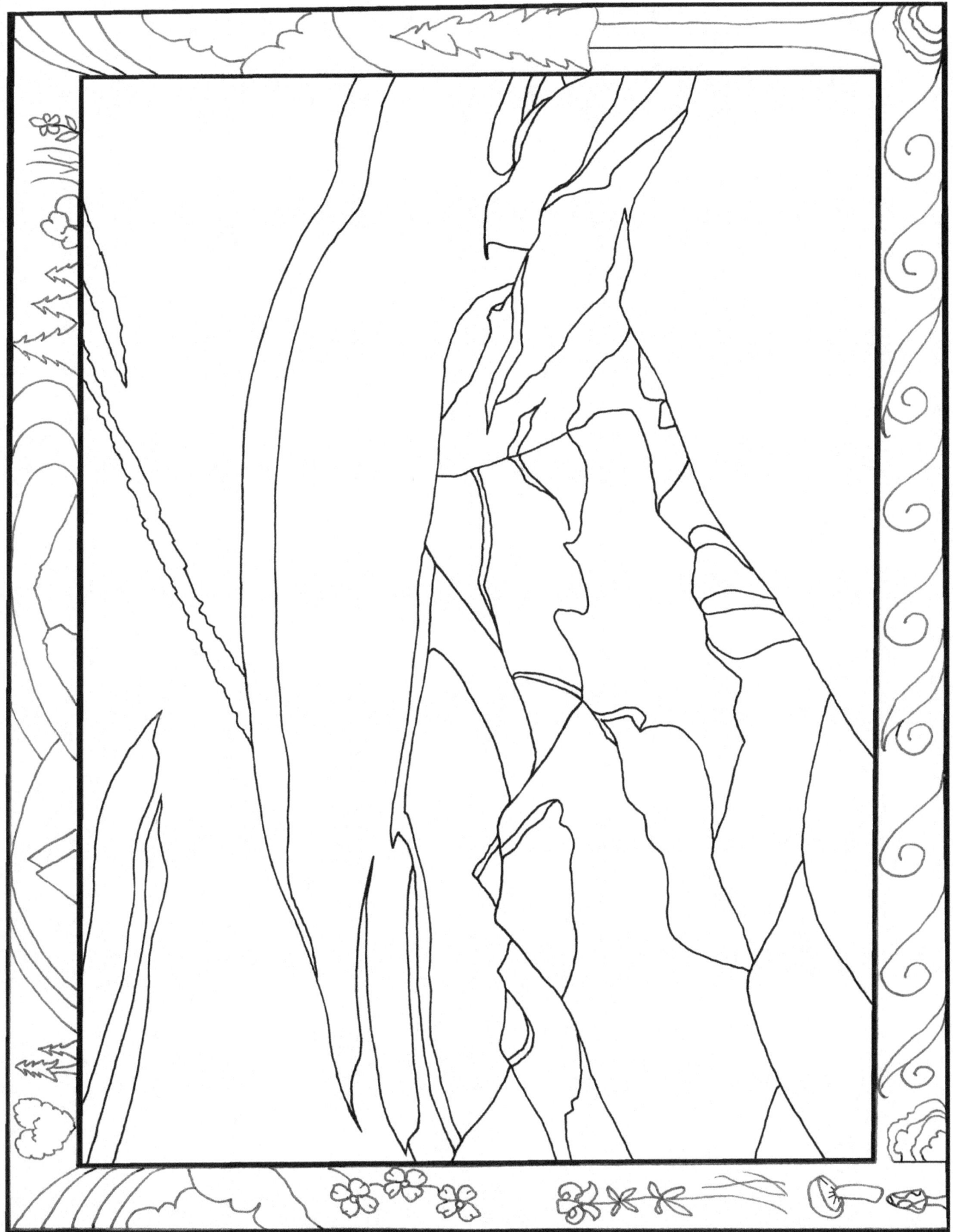

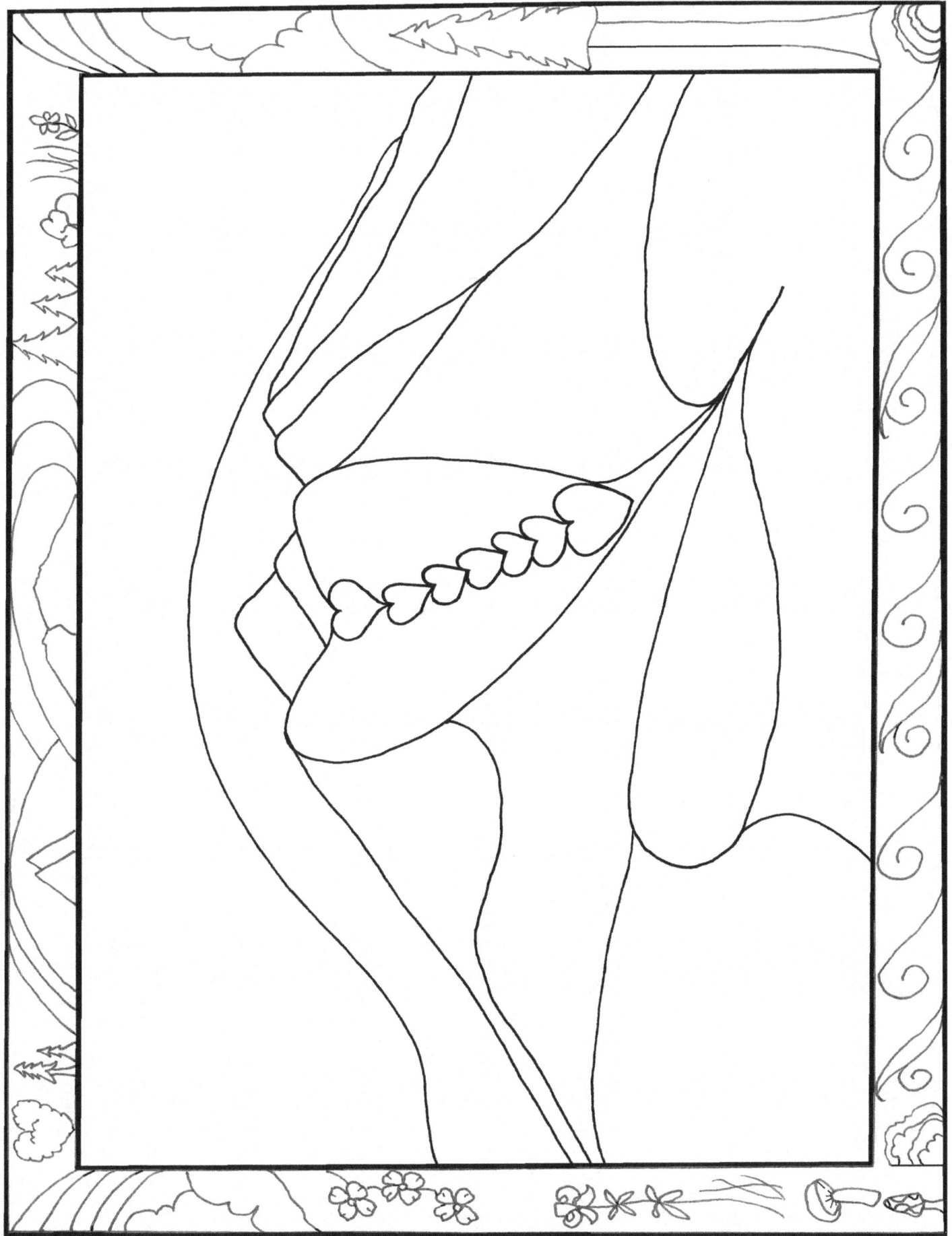

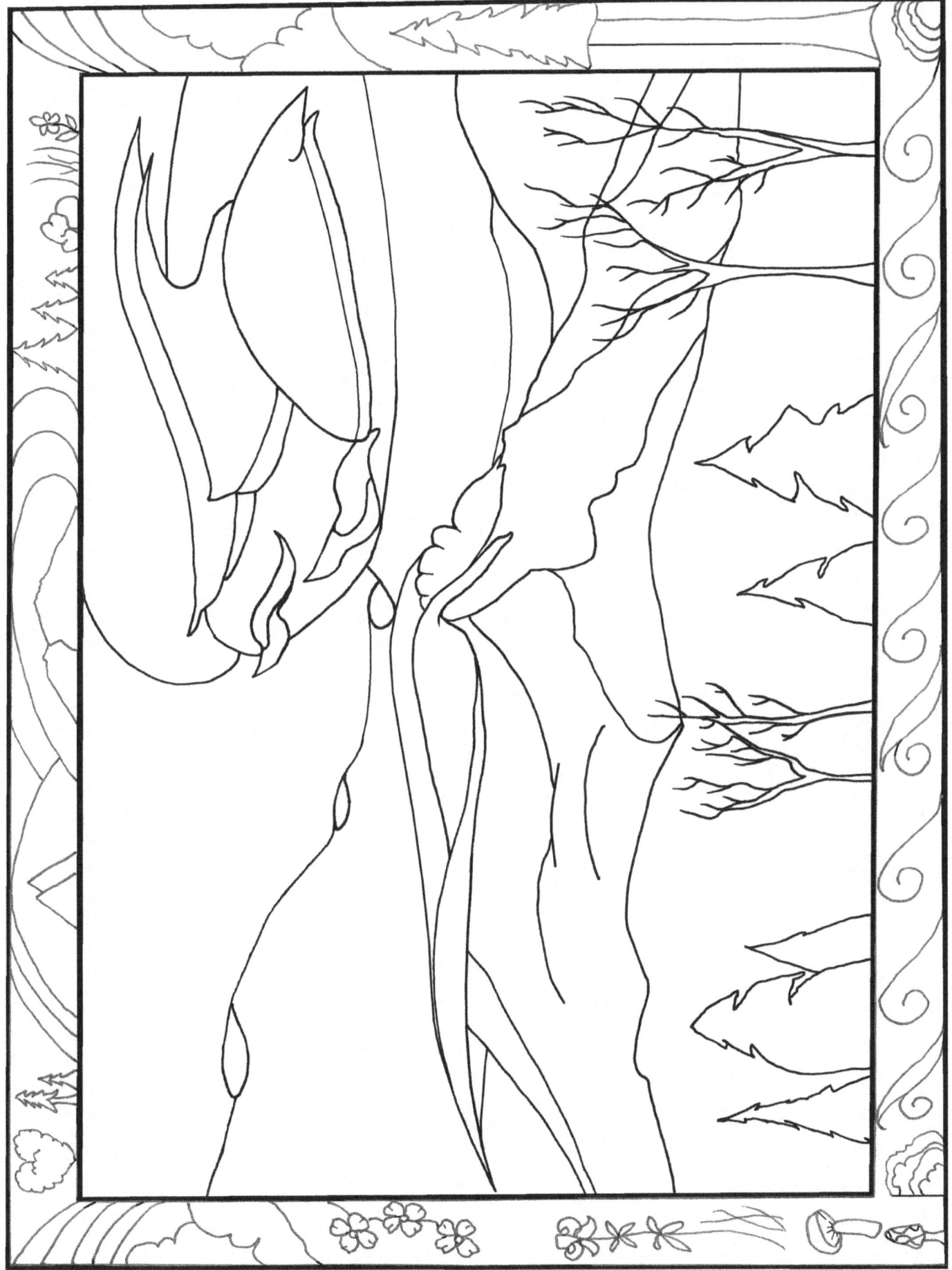

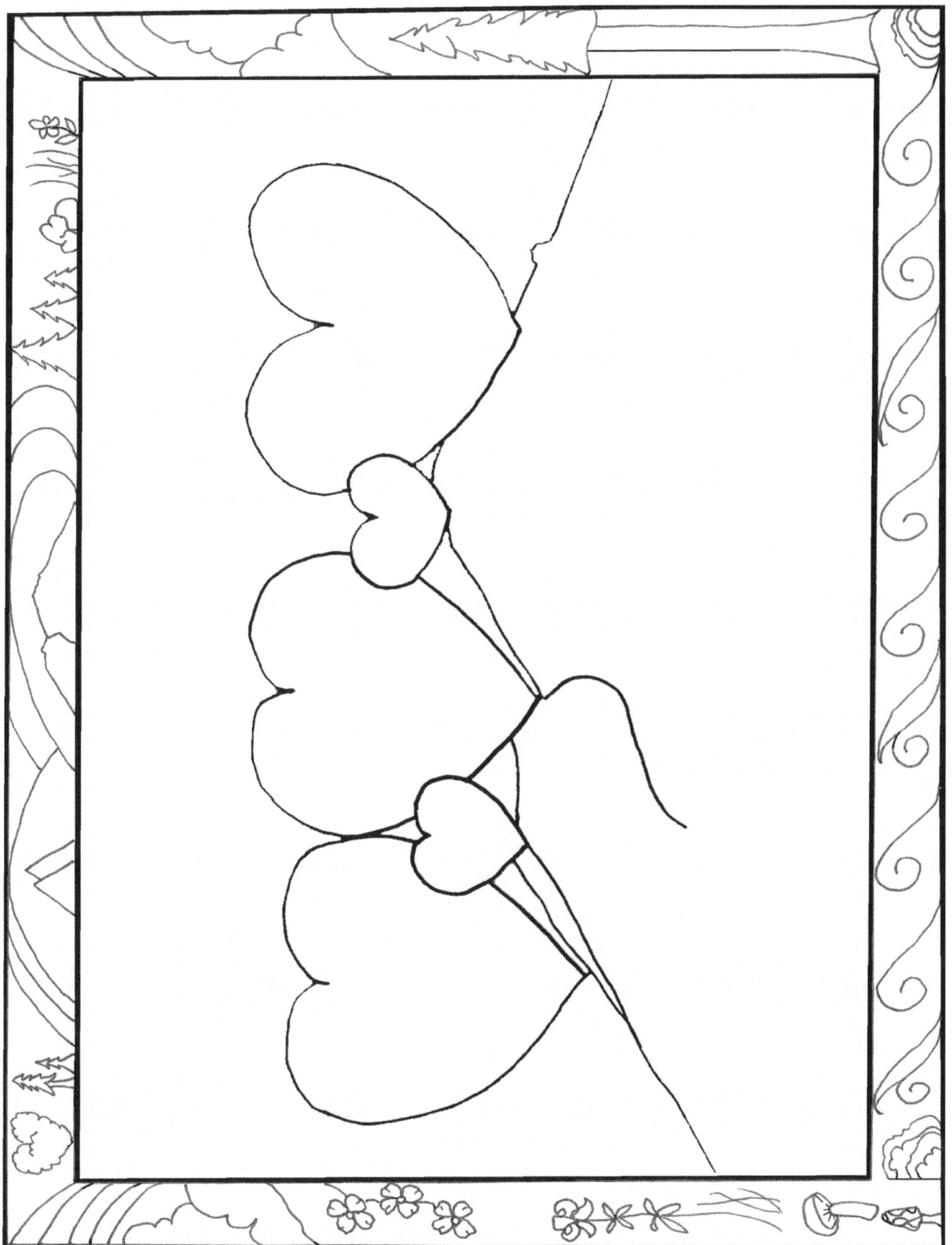

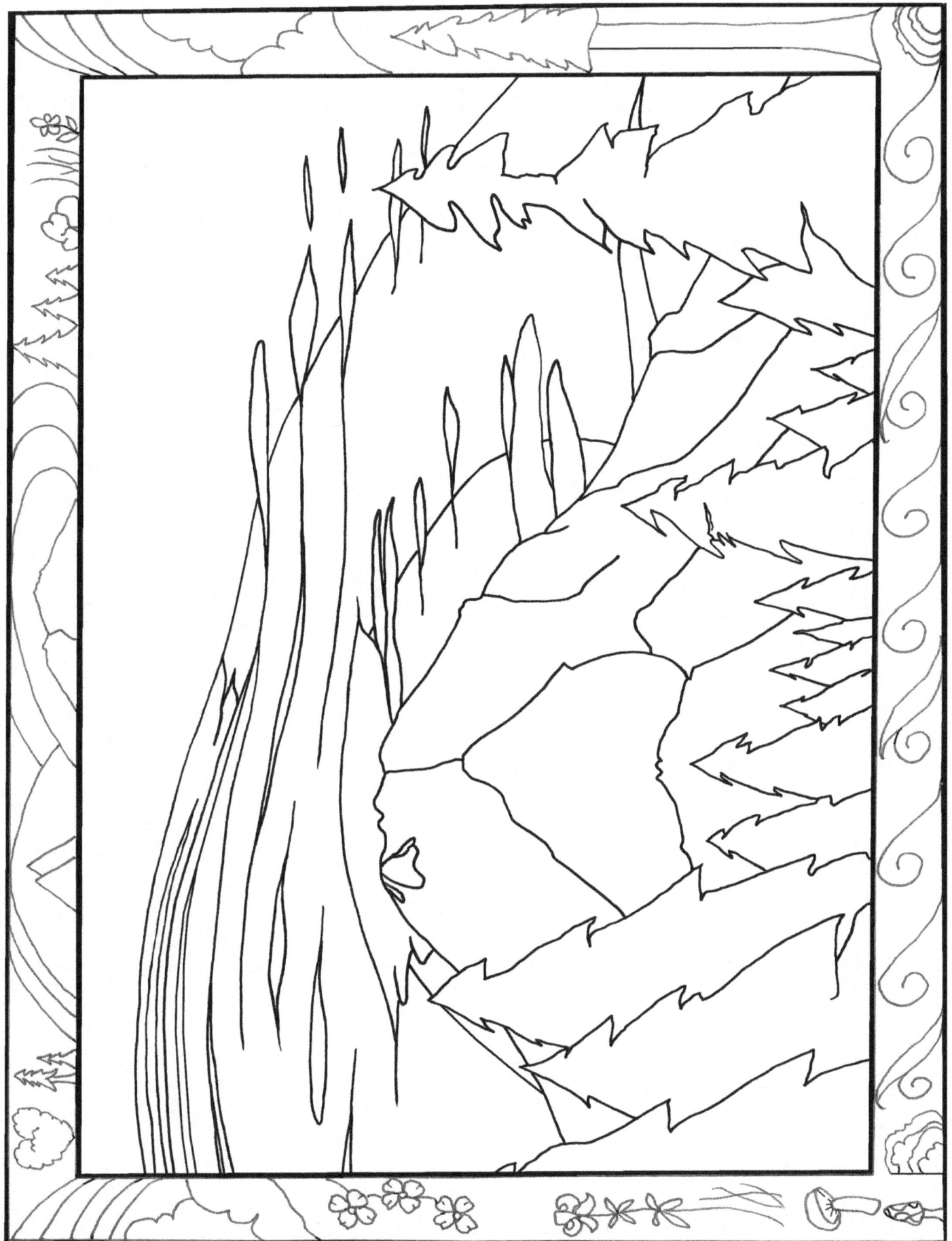

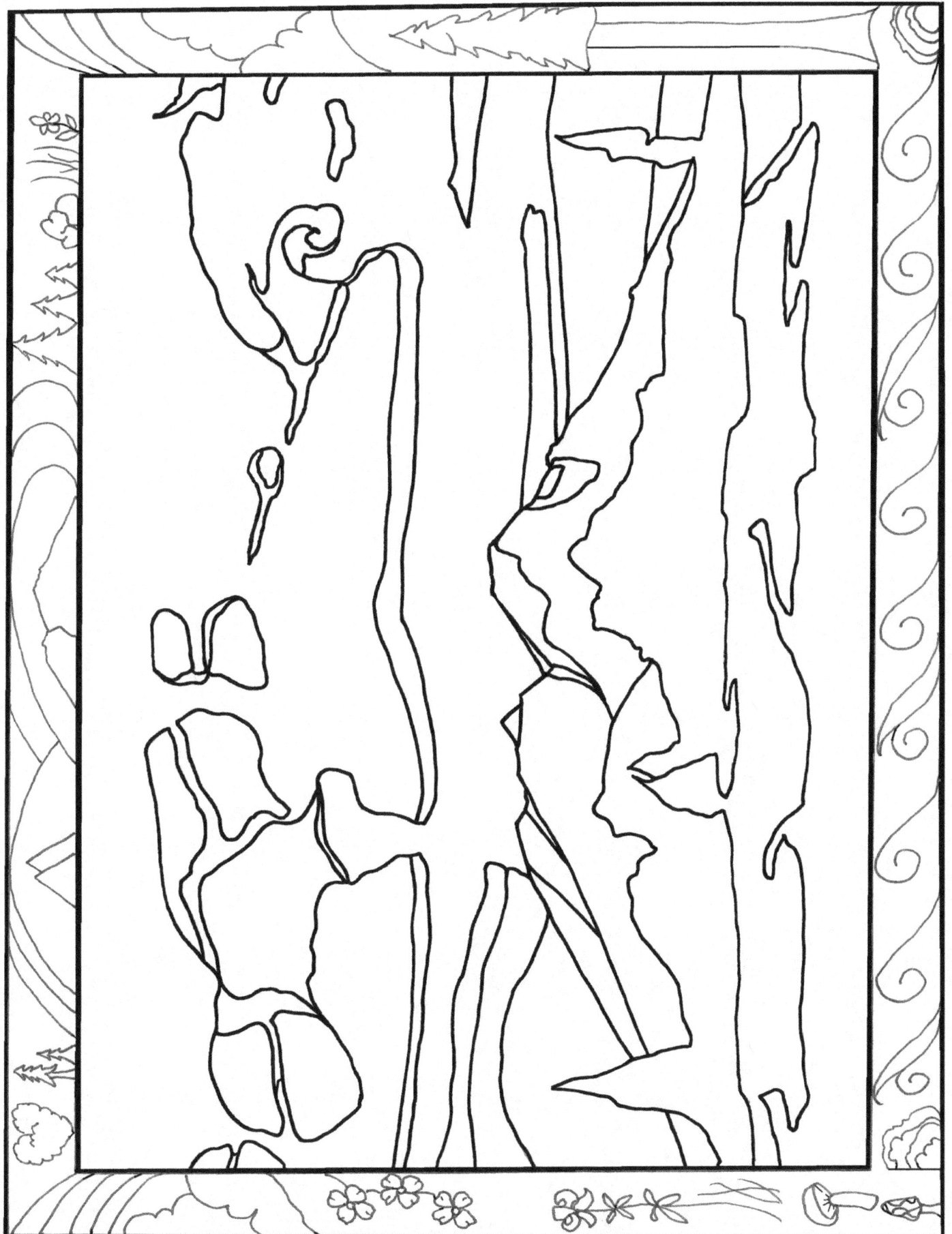

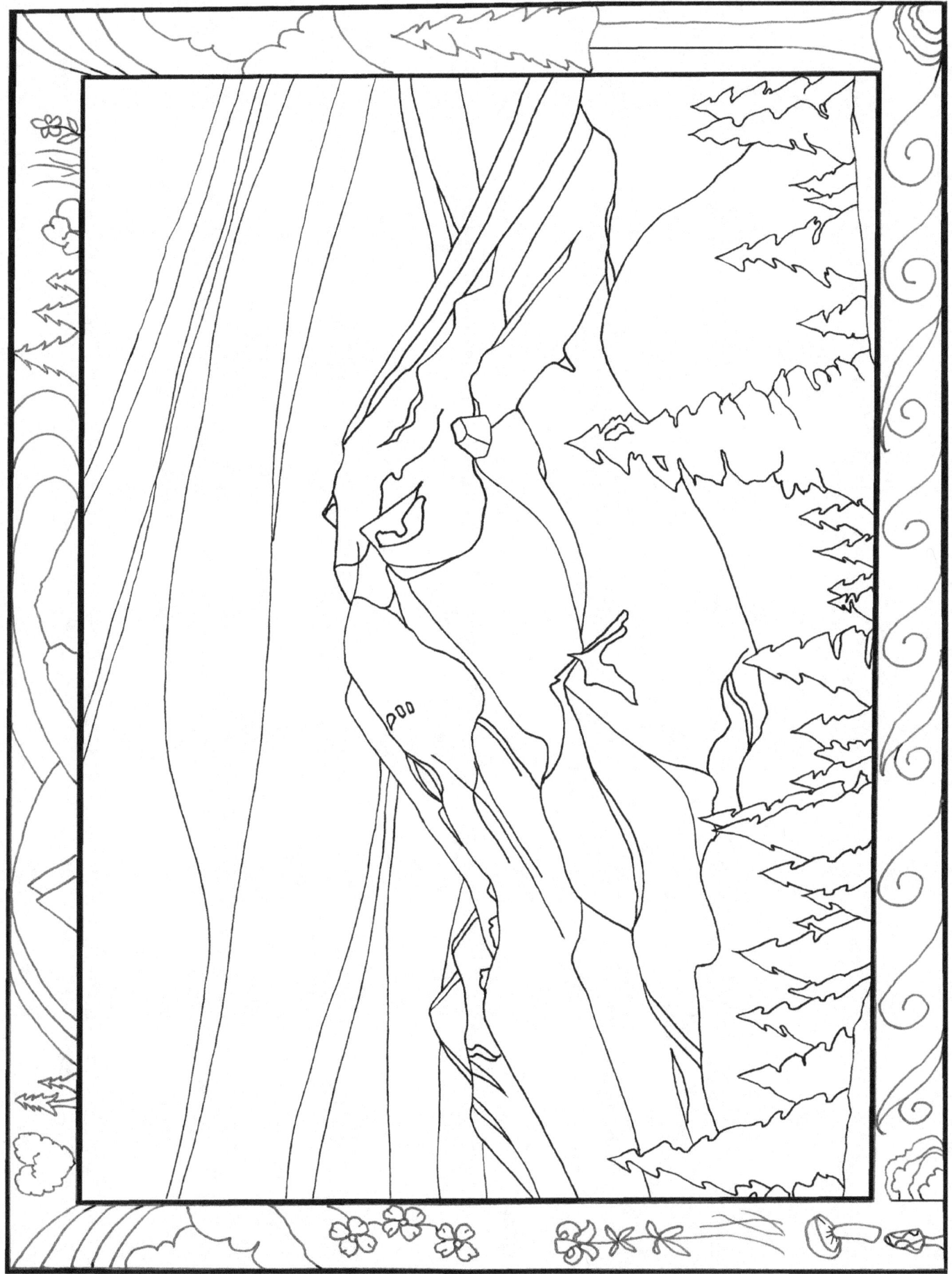

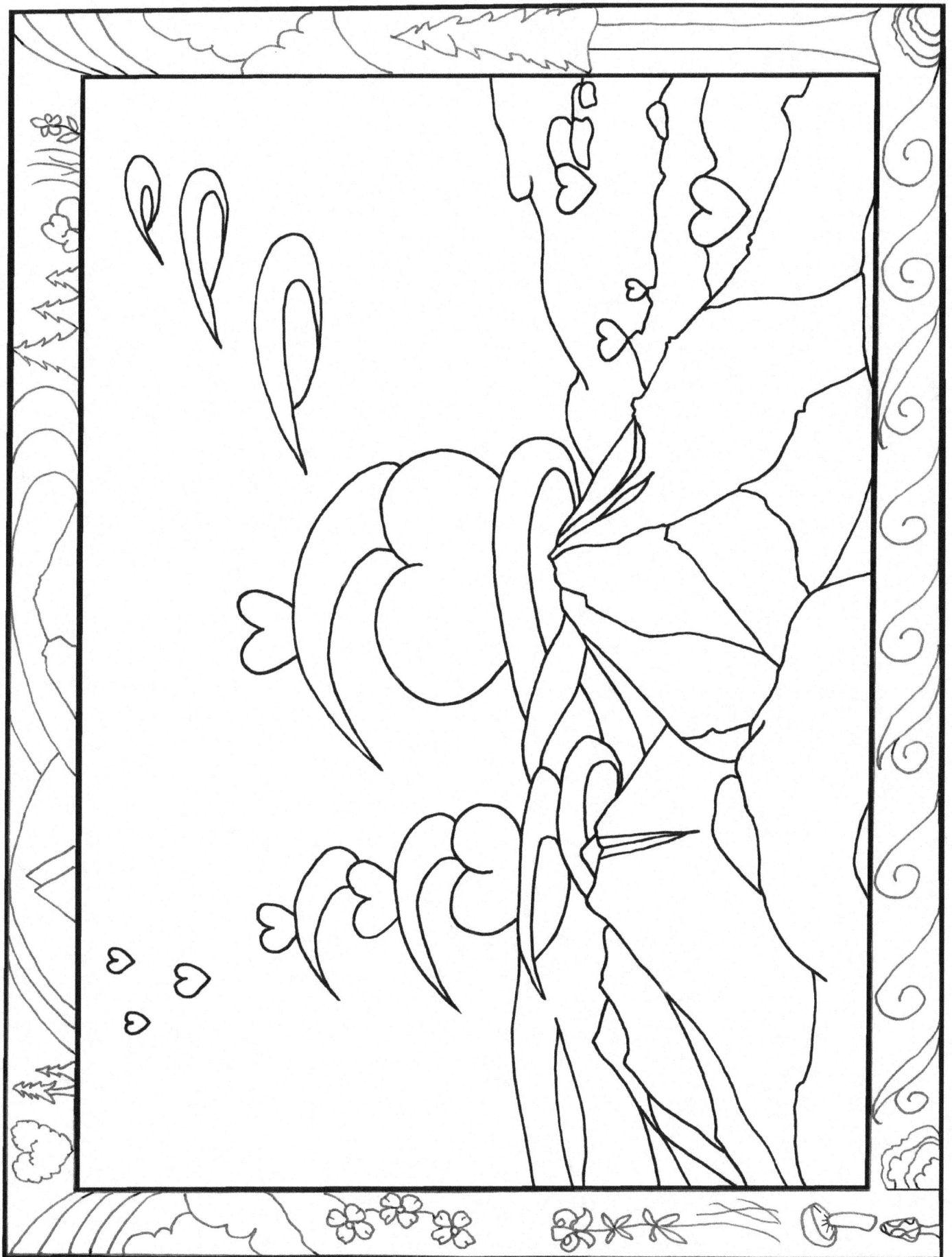

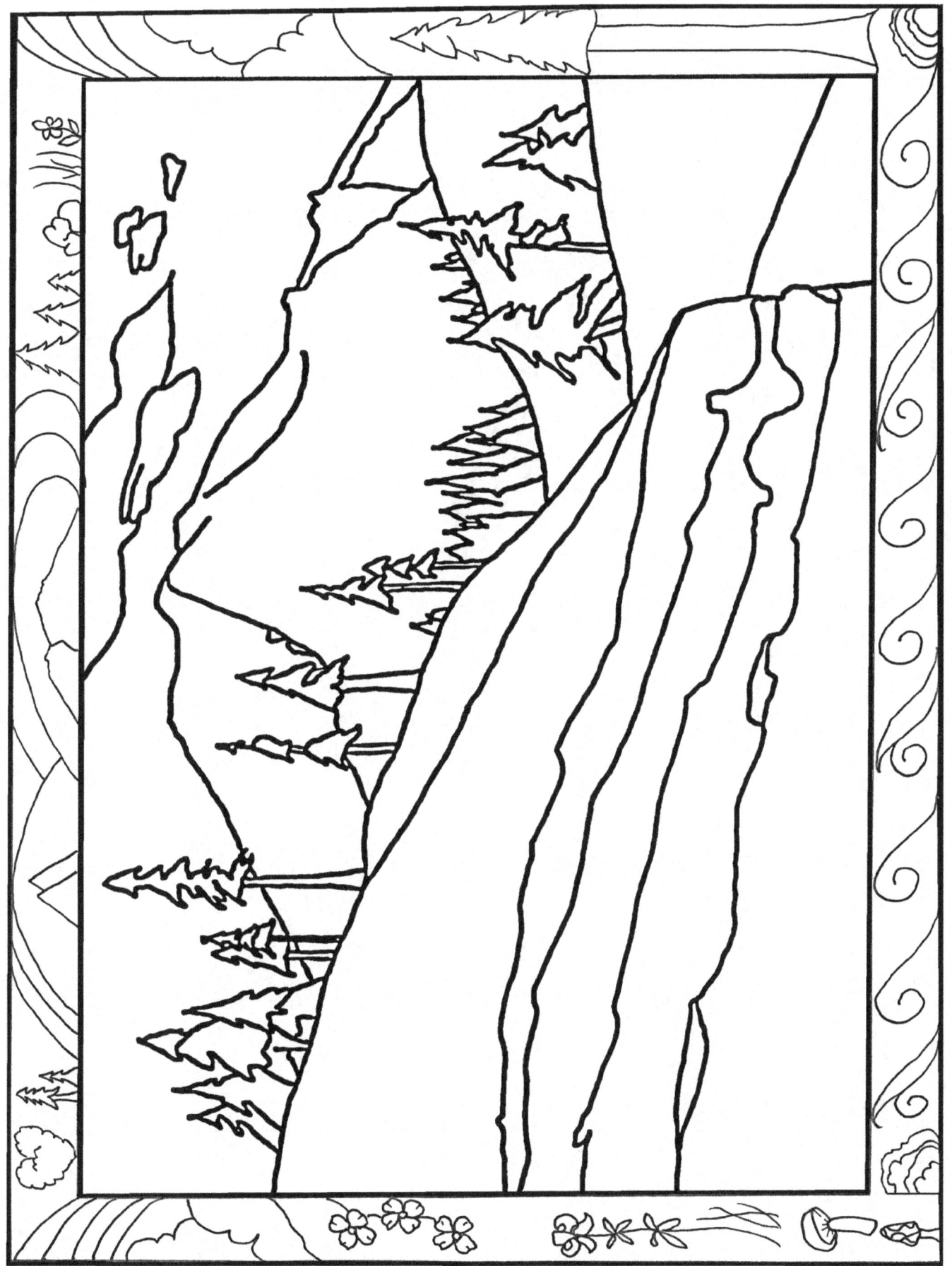

P. 24

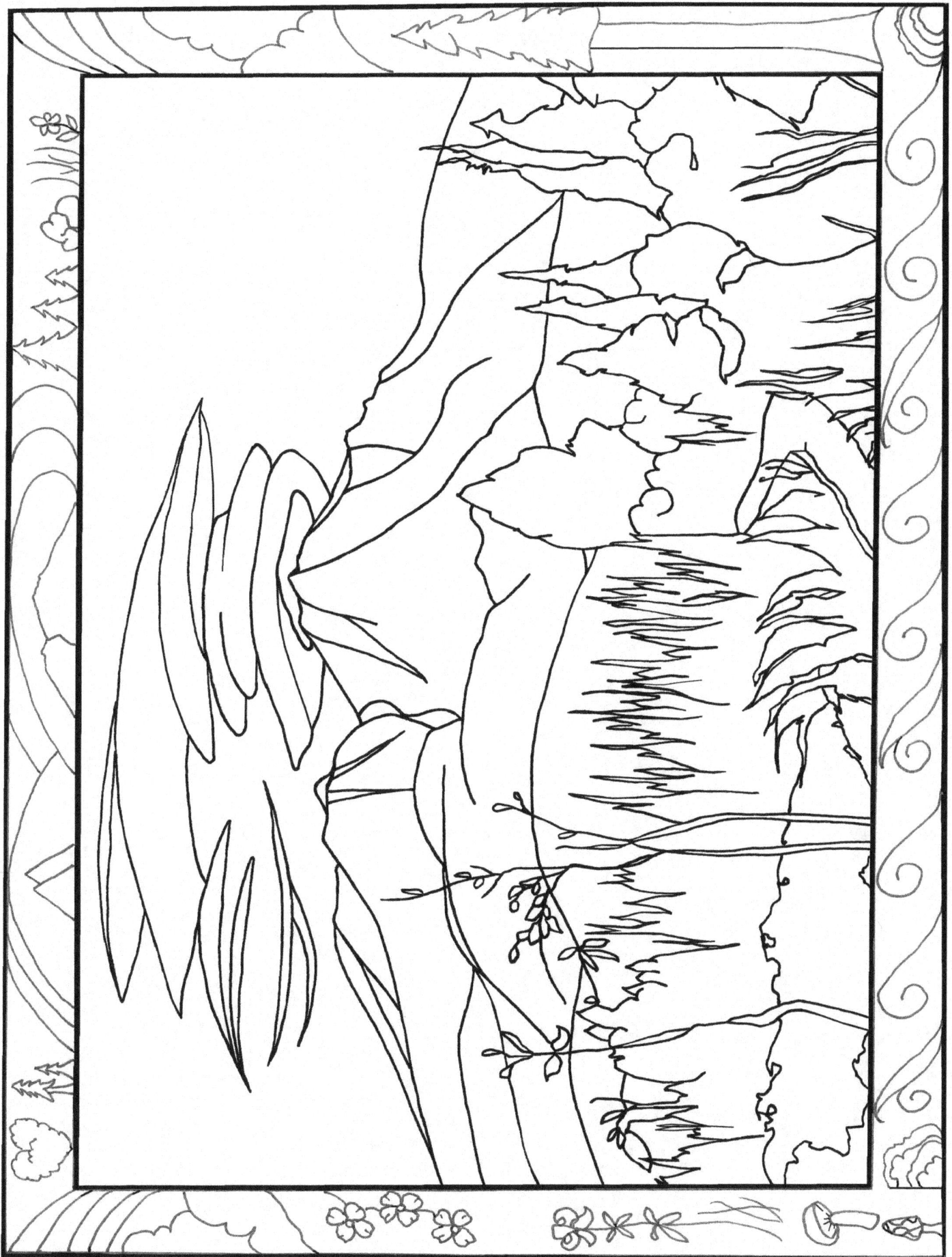

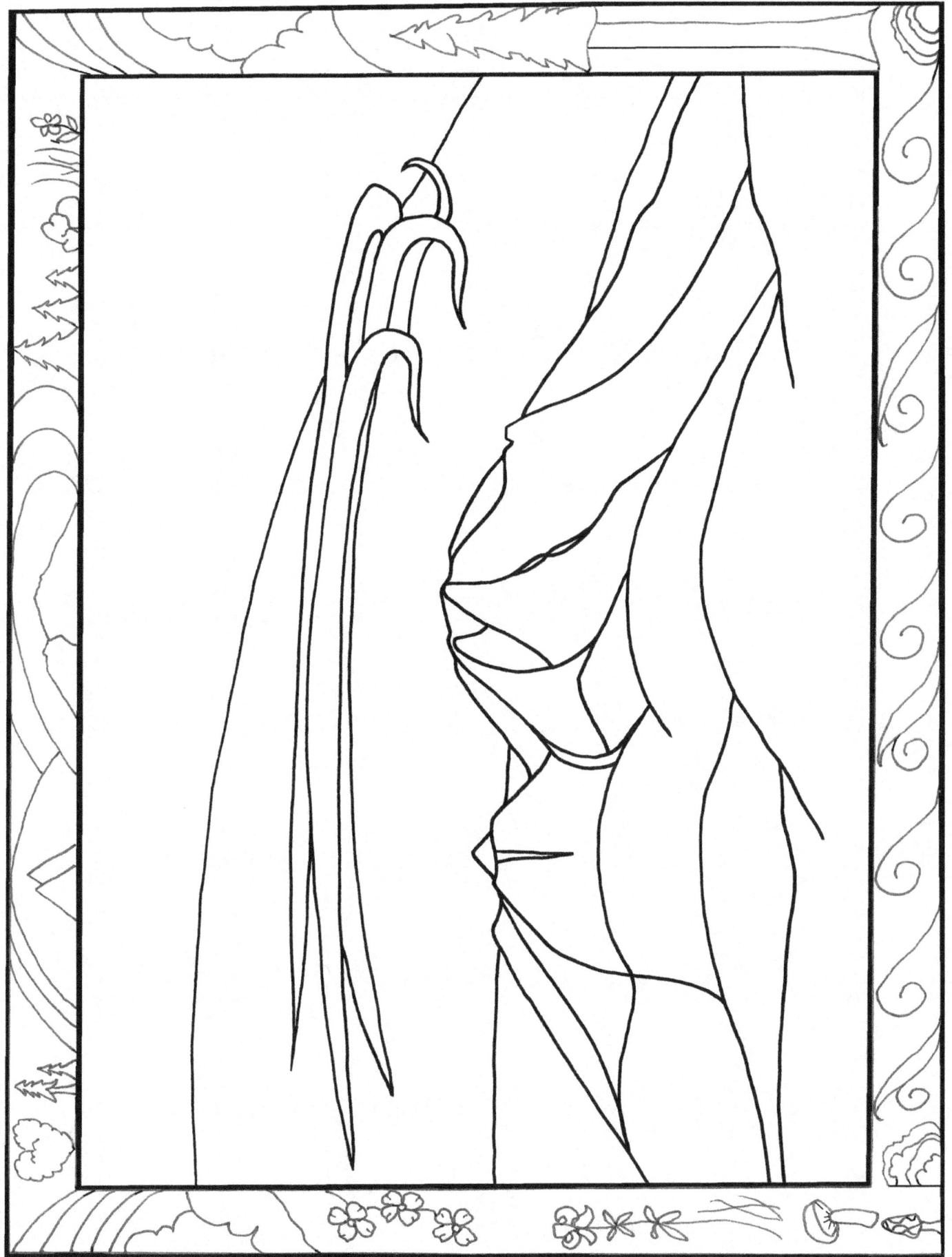

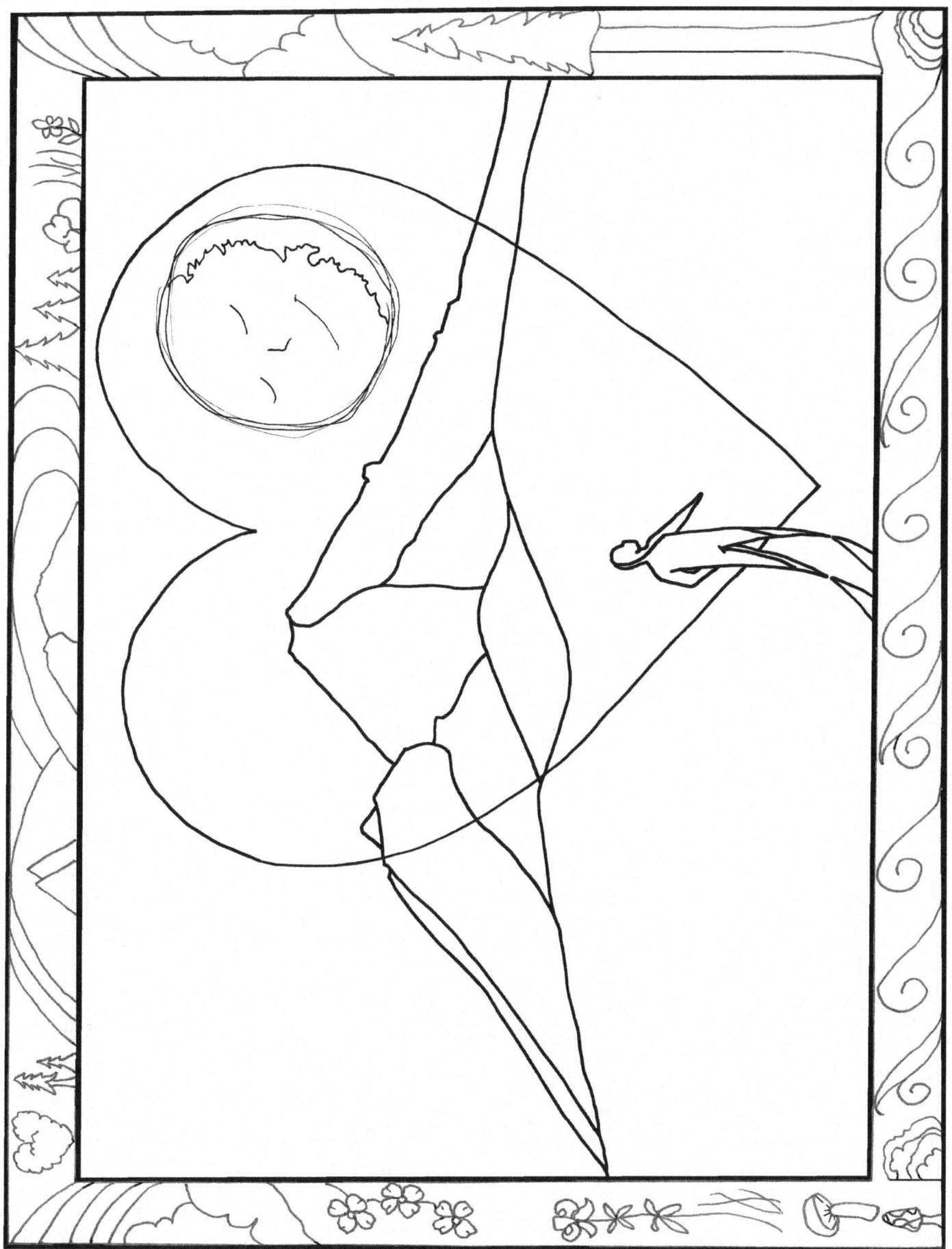

` BLOTTER PAGE `

REMOVE FROM BOOK TO USE THIS BLOTTER PAGE BETWEEN COLOR PAGES

www.ingramcontent.com/pod-product-compliance
Lightning Source LLC
Chambersburg PA
CBHW081100240526
45465CB00025B/2794